BOOSEY & HAWKES PIANO EDITIONS

LEONARD BERNSTEIN

Selected Anniversaries for Piano

EDITED BY MICHAEL MIZRAHI
with added fingering by the editor

Includes access to video piano lessons
with editor Michael Mizrahi addressing
topics in 16 of Bernstein's Anniversaries.

To access companion video piano lessons online, visit:
www.halleonard.com/mylibrary

Enter Code
8279-1531-1113-4446

ISBN 978-1-5400-2440-4

The Name and Likeness of "Leonard Bernstein" is a registered trademark of Amerbson Holdings LLC.
Used by Permission

LEONARD
BERNSTEIN
Music Publishing
Company LLC

BOOSEY&HAWKES

DISTRIBUTED BY
HAL•LEONARD®

Visit Hal Leonard Online at
www.leonardbernstein.com   **www.halleonard.com**   www.boosey.com

Contact Us:
Hal Leonard
7777 West Bluemound Road
Milwaukee, WI 53213
Email: info@halleonard.com

In Europe contact:
Hal Leonard Europe Limited
Distribution Centre, Newmarket Road
Bury St Edmunds, Suffolk, IP33 3YB
Email: info@halleonardeurope.com

In Australia contact:
Hal Leonard Australia Pty. Ltd.
4 Lentara Court
Cheltenham, Victoria, 3192 Australia
Email: info@halleonard.com.au

ALSO AVAILABLE

Leonard Bernstein: Music for Piano

Boosey & Hawkes   48020775

CONTENTS

Four Anniversaries

Five Anniversaries

Seven Anniversaries

Thirteen Anniversaries

Four Sabras

Music for the Dance, No. II

Non Troppo Presto

Sonata

Touches

Bridal Suite

CONTENTS

Eleven short video lessons accompany this edition. In some of the video lessons, I cover general topics that apply to playing several of the Anniversaries. I also chose to highlight several specific Anniversaries in order to guide students and teachers towards an approach to technical and musical challenges found in those particular pieces. In several of the videos, I give suggestions on how to practice specific passages. I tried to strike a balance between covering technically simpler Anniversaries and those requiring a more advanced technique.

Four of the video lessons focus on more general topics: "Playing Orchestrally," "Rhythm and Pulse," "Pedaling," and "Fingering." In Bernstein's piano music we must always try to bring out orchestral colors in our sound. Similarly, much of Bernstein's music features rhythm and pulse as a dominant characteristic. Finally, I examine how pedaling and fingering can steer us closer to drawing out Bernstein's musical conceptions.

Although my examples are drawn from specific passages in the music, many of my comments will be applicable to similar passages found in other Anniversaries. I encourage you to watch the short video lessons even if the piece you are working on is not covered in the video lessons.

Michael Mizrahi,
editor

Lesson 1: Playing Orchestrally
music examples from
In Memoriam: Alfred Eisner
In Memoriam: Helen Coates
For Susanna Kyle

Lesson 2: Rhythm and Pulse
music examples from
For William Schuman
For Shirley Gabis Rhoads Perle
For Johnny Mehegan

Lesson 3: Pedaling
music examples from
For Felicia Montealegre
For Aaron Copland
For Lukas Foss

Lesson 4: Fingering
music examples from
For Felicia Montealegre
For Aaron Copland
In Memoriam: Nathalie Koussetvitzky

Lesson 5: In Memoriam: Ellen Goetz

Lesson 6: For Leo Smit

Lesson 7: In Memoriam: Alfred Eisner

Lesson 8: In Memoriam: Nathalie Koussevitzky

Lesson 9: For Elizabeth Rudolf

Lesson 10: For Felicia Montealegre

Lesson 11: For Johnny Mehegan

The price of this publication includes access to companion video piano lessons, online, for download or streaming, using the unique code printed inside the book. Visit **www.halleonard.com/mylibrary** and enter the access code.

Leonard Bernstein (August 25, 1918–October 14, 1990) was born in Lawrence, Massachusetts. He took piano lessons as a boy and attended the Garrison and Boston Latin Schools. At Harvard University, he studied with Walter Piston, Edward Burlingame-Hill, and A. Tillman Merritt, among others. Before graduating in 1939, he made an unofficial conducting debut with his own incidental music to *The Birds,* and directed and performed in Marc Blitstein's *The Cradle Will Rock.* Then at the Curtis Institute of Music in Philadelphia, he studied piano with Isabella Vengerova, conducting with Fritz Reiner, and orchestration with Randall Thompson.

In 1940, he studied at the Boston Symphony Orchestra's newly created summer institute, Tanglewood, with the orchestra's conductor, Serge Koussevitzky. Bernstein later became Koussevitzky's conducting assistant. Bernstein was appointed to his first permanent conducting post in 1943, as Assistant Conductor of the New York Philharmonic. On November 14, 1943, Bernstein substituted on a few hours' notice for the ailing Bruno Walter at a Carnegie Hall concert, which was broadcast nationally on radio, receiving critical acclaim. Soon orchestras worldwide sought him out as a guest conductor.

In 1945 he was appointed Music Director of the New York City Symphony Orchestra, a post he held until 1947. After Serge Koussevitzky died in 1951, Bernstein headed the orchestral and conducting departments at Tanglewood, teaching there for many years. In 1951 he married the Chilean actress and pianist, Felicia Montealegre. He was also visiting music professor, and head of the Creative Arts Festivals at Brandeis University in the early 1950s.

Bernstein became Music Director of the New York Philharmonic in 1958. From then until 1969 he led more concerts with the orchestra than any previous conductor. He subsequently held the lifetime title of Laureate Conductor, making frequent guest appearances with the orchestra. More than half of Bernstein's 400-plus recordings were made with the New York Philharmonic.

Bernstein traveled the world as a conductor. Immediately after World War II, in 1946, he conducted in London and at the International Music Festival in Prague. In 1947 he conducted in Tel Aviv, beginning a relationship with Israel that lasted until his death. In 1953, Bernstein was the first American to conduct opera at the Teatro alla Scala in Milan: Cherubini's *Medea* with Maria Callas.

Bernstein was a leading advocate of American composers, particularly Aaron Copland. The two remained close friends for life. As a young pianist, Bernstein performed Copland's *Piano Variations* so often he considered the composition his trademark. Bernstein programmed and recorded nearly all of the Copland orchestral works—many of them twice. He devoted several televised *Young People's Concerts* to Copland, and gave the premiere of Copland's *Connotations,* commissioned for the opening of Philharmonic Hall (now Avery Fisher Hall) at Lincoln Center in 1962.

While Bernstein's conducting repertoire encompassed the standard literature, he may be best remembered for his performances and recordings of Haydn, Beethoven, Brahms, Schumann, Sibelius and Mahler. Particularly notable were his performances of the Mahler symphonies with the New York Philharmonic in the 1960s, sparking a renewed interest in the works of Mahler.

Inspired by his Jewish heritage, Bernstein completed his first large-scale work: *Symphony No. 1: Jeremiah* (1943). The piece was first performed with the Pittsburgh Symphony Orchestra in 1944, conducted by the composer, and received the New York Music Critics' Award. Koussevitzky premiered Bernstein's *Symphony No. 2: The Age of Anxiety* with the Boston Symphony Orchestra, Bernstein as piano soloist. His *Symphony No. 3: Kaddish*, composed in 1963, was premiered by the Israel Philharmonic Orchestra. Kaddish is dedicated "To the Beloved Memory of John F. Kennedy."

Other major compositions by Bernstein include *Prelude, Fugue and Riffs* for solo clarinet and jazz ensemble (1949); *Serenade* for violin, strings and percussion, (1954); *Symphonic Dances from West Side Story*, (1960); *Chichester Psalms* for chorus, boy soprano and orchestra (1965); *Mass: A Theater Piece for Singers, Players and Dancers*, commissioned for the opening of the John F. Kennedy Center for the Performing Arts in Washington, DC, and first produced there in 1971; *Songfest* a song cycle for six singers and orchestra (1977); *Divertimento*, for orchestra (1980); *Halil*, for solo flute and small orchestra (1981); *Touches*, for solo piano (1981); *Missa Brevis* for singers and percussion (1988); *Thirteen Anniversaries* for solo piano (1988); *Concerto for Orchestra: Jubilee Games*, (1989); and *Arias and Barcarolles* for two singers and piano duet (1988).

Bernstein also wrote a one-act opera, *Trouble in Tahiti*, in 1952, and its sequel, the three-act opera, *A Quiet Place* in 1983. He collaborated with choreographer Jerome Robbins on three major ballets: *Fancy Free*

(1944) and *Facsimile* (1946) for the American Ballet theater; and *Dybbuk* (1975) for the New York City Ballet. He composed the score for the award-winning movie *On the Waterfront* (1954) and incidental music for two Broadway plays: *Peter Pan* (1950) and *The Lark* (1955).

Bernstein contributed substantially to the Broadway musical stage. He collaborated with Betty Comden and Adolph Green on *On The Town* (1944) and *Wonderful Town* (1953). In collaboration with Richard Wilbur and Lillian Hellman and others he wrote *Candide* (1956). Other versions of *Candide* were written in association with Hugh Wheeler, Stephen Sondheim, et al. In 1957 he again collaborated with Jerome Robbins, Stephen Sondheim, and Arthur Laurents, on the landmark musical *West Side Story*, also made into the Academy Award-winning film. In 1976 Bernstein and Alan Jay Lerner wrote *1600 Pennsylvania Avenue*.

Festivals of Bernstein's music have been produced throughout the world. In 1978 the Israel Philharmonic sponsored a festival commemorating his years of dedication to Israel. The Israel Philharmonic also bestowed on him the lifetime title of Laureate Conductor in 1988. In 1986 the London Symphony Orchestra and the Barbican Centre produced a Bernstein Festival. The London Symphony Orchestra in 1987 named him Honorary President. In 1989 the city of Bonn presented a Beethoven/Bernstein Festival.

In 1985 the National Academy of Recording Arts and Sciences honored Mr. Bernstein with the Lifetime Achievement Grammy Award. He won eleven Emmy Awards and the Antoinette Perry Award for Distinguished Achievement in the Theater. His televised concert and lecture series started with the Omnibus program in 1954, followed by the extraordinary *Young People's Concerts with the New York Philharmonic*, in 1958 that extended over fourteen seasons. Among his many appearances on the PBS series *Great Performances* was the eleven-part acclaimed "Bernstein's Beethoven." In 1989, Bernstein and others commemorated the 1939 invasion of Poland in a worldwide telecast from Warsaw.

Bernstein's writings were published in *The Joy of Music* (1959), *Leonard Bernstein's Young People's Concerts* (1961), *The Infinite Variety of Music* (1966), and *Findings* (1982). Each has been widely translated. He gave six lectures at Harvard University in 1972–73 as the Charles Eliot Norton Professor of Poetry. These lectures were subsequently published and televised as *The Unanswered Question*.

Bernstein always rejoiced in opportunities to teach young musicians. His master classes at Tanglewood were famous. He was instrumental in founding the Los Angeles Philharmonic Institute in 1982. He helped create a world class training orchestra at the Schleswig Holstein Music Festival. He founded the Pacific Music Festival in Sapporo, Japan. Modeled after Tanglewood, this international festival was the first of its kind in Asia and continues to this day.

Bernstein received many honors. He was elected in 1981 to the American Academy of Arts and Letters, which gave him a Gold Medal. The National Fellowship Award in 1985 applauded his life-long support of humanitarian causes. He received the MacDowell Colony's Gold Medal; medals from the Beethoven Society and the Mahler Gesellschaft; the Handel Medallion, New York City's highest honor for the arts; a Tony award (1969) for Distinguished Achievement in the Theater; and dozens of honorary degrees and awards from colleges and universities. He was presented ceremonial keys to the cities of Oslo, Vienna, Bersheeva and the village of Bernstein, Austria, among others. National honors came from Italy, Israel, Mexico, Denmark, Germany (the Great Merit Cross), and France (Chevalier, Officer and Commandeur of the Legion d'Honneur). He received the Kennedy Center Honors in 1980.

World peace was a particular concern of Bernstein. Speaking at Johns Hopkins University in 1980 and the Cathedral of St. John the Divine in New York in 1983, he described his vision of global harmony. His "Journey for Peace" tour to Athens and Hiroshima with the European Community Orchestra in 1985, commemorated the 40th anniversary of the atom bomb. In December 1989, Bernstein conducted the historic "Berlin Celebration Concerts" on both sides of the Berlin Wall, as it was being dismantled. The concerts were unprecedented gestures of cooperation, the musicians representing the former East Germany, West Germany, and the four powers that had partitioned Berlin after World War II.

Bernstein supported Amnesty International from its inception. To benefit the effort, he established the Felicia Montealegre Fund in 1987 in memory of his wife who passed away in 1978. In 1990, Bernstein received the Praemium Imperiale, an international prize created in 1988 by the Japan Arts Association and awarded for lifetime achievement in the arts. Bernstein used the $100,000 prize to establish The Bernstein Education Through the Arts (BETA) Fund, Inc. before his death on October 14, 1990.

Bernstein was the father of three children—Jamie, Alexander, and Nina—and the grandfather of four: Francisca, Evan, Anya, and Anna.

– reprinted by permission of Boosey & Hawkes

BERNSTEIN AND THE PIANO

For a composer who declared the keyboard to be his "first love," it is curious that Leonard Bernstein wrote as little as he did for the piano.[1] Bernstein's works for solo keyboard are generally modest affairs, presenting one or two amiable themes and spinning them out simply across a couple of minutes of music. These miniatures are of a vastly smaller scale than his large symphonic works (*Jeremiah Symphony*, *Chichester Psalms*, *Serenade after Plato's "Symposium"*) which are firmly established in the orchestral repertory, and for good reason.

However, these underperformed piano works reveal a Bernstein every bit as tuneful, spirited, and emotionally direct as the Bernstein of *West Side Story*, *Candide*, and *Mass*. Each of these distilled miniatures explores a single mood, sometimes with a sense of improvisatory freedom, always with a conciseness of expression and unfailing sense for how to make the piano sing and dance.

In his teenage years, Bernstein spent hours a day at the piano, studying with Boston's leading piano teachers, and giving several important formative performances on the piano. So why didn't he write more for solo keyboard? For one thing, by his own admission, Bernstein loved being around people. By the late 1930s, the time of Bernstein's undergraduate years at Harvard, it was clear that his talents lay in mounting large-scale productions, and that his musical career would not center around the solitary solo piano (either as performer or composer).

Of course, in writing each of these Anniversaries for specific people, Bernstein has surrounded himself with his friends and mentors even while alone at the keyboard. And, as it turns out, several of the Anniversaries share musical material found in his major symphonic works, most notably the *Serenade after Plato's "Symposium."* Thus, these solo piano works provide both a brilliant reflection of the public life of Bernstein the symphonic composer and a telling glimpse into the private life of Bernstein the teacher, mentor, student, and friend.

GENERAL BACKGROUND ON THE ANNIVERSARIES

Most of Bernstein's compositions for solo piano took the form of the Anniversary. Bernstein is not the first composer to have written a short homage to commemorate a special date; he perhaps took his inspiration from Virgil Thompson (1896–1989) and that composer's *Portraits*. Bernstein wrote a total of 29 Anniversaries spanning virtually the entirety of his creative life, from the early 1940s until the late 1980s. Each of the Anniversaries were written in honor of someone in Bernstein's life: mentors, friends, students, teachers. Except for those cited as "In Memoriam," the Anniversaries were birthday presents, and thus, the honoree's birthday was included with the title.

The first set was *Seven Anniversaries* (composed 1942–43, premiered by the composer in 1943). Five of these are included in the present collection. **Aaron Copland** (1900–1990), the eminent American composer 18 years Bernstein's senior, was one of his earliest mentors.[2] **Alfred Eisner** (1916–1941) was a former roommate and close friend at Harvard in the late 1930s who died very young of cancer. **Sergei Koussevitzky** (1874–1951) was a famed conductor and another of Bernstein's early mentors. **Nathalie Koussevitzky** (1880–1942) was Sergei's second wife; a fund established in her honor after her death commissioned Bernstein's *Serenade after Plato's "Symposium"* (see below). **William Schuman** (1910–1992) was a composer and President of the Lincoln Center for the Performing Arts while Bernstein was conductor of the New York Philharmonic. In his 1982 book *Findings*, Bernstein refers to Copland and Sergei Koussevitzky as his "musical fathers."[3]

In 1948, Bernstein composed his *Four Anniversaries*, premiered in that same year by Eudice Podis. Two of these are included here. **Felicia Montealegre** (1922–1978) was a Chilean pianist and actor, and Bernstein's wife until her death. **Johnny Mehegan** (1916–1984) was a jazz pianist who had impressed Bernstein with his freewheeling improvisations in a New York City nightclub.

The *Five Anniversaries* were composed 1949–51. Three of these are included here. The son of **Elizabeth Rudolf** (1894–????) studied with Bernstein at the Tanglewood Music Center in western Massachusetts.[4] **Lukas**

---

1 Bernstein dedicated his 1981 piano work *Touches* "to my first love, the keyboard."

2 Aaron Copland's *Piano Variations* were a major influence on Bernstein, both as pianist and composer. Bernstein impressed Copland with his brash reading of the elder composer's score at a party on the day they met, November 14, 1937.

3 *Findings*, Preface.

4 In 2018 in an informal coversation, Berstein's daughter Jamie recalled that Elizabeth Rudolph was "the mother of Bernstein's fellow Tanglewood student, Gus Rudolph. On several occasions when my father was traveling out west with Gus, he had occasion to stay at the Rudolph's ranch in Wyoming, so this piece must have been a thank-you present to Mrs. Rudolph for her hospitality"

Foss (1922–2009) was a composer, pianist, conductor, and close friend of Bernstein's from their student days at the Curtis Institute of Music in Philadelphia and at Tanglewood. **Susanna Kyle** (1949–????) was the daughter of Betty Comden, who collaborated with Bernstein in a number of highly successful theater productions, including *On the Town*.

The set of *Thirteen Anniversaries* was compiled in 1988 from material composed by Bernstein between the early 1960s and the late 1980s. Six are included here. **Shirley Gabis Rhoads Perle** (b. 1924) was a lifelong friend of Bernstein's from when he was a student at Curtis in the early 1940s. **Stephen Sondheim** (b. 1930) is the famed composer and lyricist who achieved an early career breakthrough when he partnered with Bernstein on the Broadway musical *West Side Story*. **Craig Urquhart** (b. 1953) was Bernstein's personal assistant near the end of Bernstein's life. **Leo Smit** (1921–1999) was a pianist and composer whose music and performances were championed by Bernstein. **Helen Coates** (1889–1989) was Bernstein's first influential piano teacher, in Boston in the mid 1930s, and later his personal assistant for many decades. The music from **In Memoriam: Ellen Goetz** (1930–1986) was originally set as a song (unpublished) titled "First Love (for My Mother, March 1986)," which Bernstein wrote for his mother, Jennie Resnick Bernstein, on the occasion of her 88th birthday.

Musical and technical considerations guided my selection of the specific Anniversaries included here. The pieces are presented roughly in progressive order of difficulty. In some cases, I have presented pieces back-to-back because they make a nice pairing (the two Koussevitzkys, for example). Played in order, the five pieces included here from *Seven Anniversaries* make a particularly strong set. The pair of Anniversaries from *Four Anniversaries* would likewise work well, especially for an advanced pianist.

When asked whether the Anniversaries sought to depict the personalities of their dedicatees or the sound of their music, Bernstein replied "Yes, in a general sense."[5] Bernstein's equivocal comment notwithstanding, the Anniversaries display first and foremost the sensibilities and aesthetic of Bernstein himself, a larger-than-life personality whose music bore the marked influence of his friends and mentors, fusing them together to create a unique, distinctive compositional voice.

MUSICAL MATERIAL IN THE ANNIVERSARIES

Several of the Anniversaries share musical material with other works by Bernstein.

- "In Memoriam: Ellen Goetz" appears as the "Nachtspiel" in *Arias and Barcarolles*.
- "In Memoriam: Helen Coates" is a virtual transcription of the Meditation No. 1 from the 1971 theater piece *Mass*.
- "For Susanna Kyle" appears as the Introduction to Act II in the uncut version of *Peter Pan*.
- "For Stephen Sondheim" contains material that would later be used in the first version of Bernstein's opera *A Quiet Place*.
- The Anniversaries dedicated to Elizabeth Rudolf and Lukas Foss (and two other Anniversaries from the same set not included here) include music that would be later presented as central motives in the violin concerto titled *Serenade after Plato's "Symposium."* (The Anniversary dedicated to Craig Urquhart also seems to occupy a similar sound world, even if the material is not directly quoted from the *Serenade*).
- "In Memoriam: Nathalie Koussevitzky" includes music that would appear prominently in the final section of Bernstein's first symphony, *Jeremiah*.

GENERAL PEDAGOGICAL CHALLENGES

A core challenge in playing these "tiny tributes" lays in capturing the mood of each piece with often only a few measures to do so. A singing tone is essential, song-like as many of these Anniversaries are. A sense of orchestral color is similarly essential; Bernstein was ever the symphonist, even in these works for solo piano. Finally, a strong sense of rhythm and pulse is necessary in many of the Anniversaries which are laced with explosions of jazz and Stravinskian meter changes.

Despite his training as a pianist, Bernstein's piano music often comes across as orchestral in concept, especially in those Anniversaries noted above which were later incorporated into orchestral works. In order to achieve an orchestral sound, multiple voices must sometimes be projected in the same hand, each with its own color and articulation. The performer must possess a firm finger *legato*, with numerous finger substitutions often necessary. Use pedal coloristically, from fully depressed to *senza pedale*, and everything in between.

---

5 Luther, 9–10

NOTES ON PLAYING THE SELECTED ANNIVERSARIES

In Memoriam: Helen Coates

In the original setting for this music (Meditation No. 1 from *Mass*), most of the material is performed by massed string instruments: violins, violas, cellos, and basses. The resultant sound is lushly intense, like a sustained grief-stricken cry, at first out into the world and then focused inwardly. In this version for the keyboard, play the *f* accents and *tenuto* chords with arm weight, listening actively through each melodic note (as if bowing a long note on a string instrument). Voice the hands clearly; the dissonances are even more biting if the chords are voiced well.

The repetition of so many of the same pitches within short melodic fragments can impede horizontal phrasing. For example, in the first two bars, the same E-flat is heard three times, an accent on each one. Play these three E-flats (and any set of similarly recurring notes) differently from one another. Practice playing *f* passages *mp* and without accents to get a sense for the natural phrasing, then keep that phrasing once you add in the accents.

If possible, do not roll the tenths in measures 19, 23, and 34, and hold the low G with your fifth finger (rather than the pedal). It could also be possible to "set" the low G with the middle pedal, either before you start the piece, or immediately before the measures in question (the G is not used anywhere else, and you do not need *una corda* in this piece at all).

For Aaron Copland

This Anniversary brings to mind Copland's pieces of the 1940s (*Appalachian Spring*, *Rodeo*), surely a conscious evocation on Bernstein's part. The style is one of simplicity, warmth, openness, and spontaneity. Use sparing pedal and finger *legato* to create a connected sound. Listen to long-held notes actively (such as the dyad held from measures 2–4), as if played by string or wind instruments. If possible, hold the A in measure 4 for the full three beats. Highlight the wide changes in register (as in the low octaves entering in measure 4). Color surprise harmonic shifts, such as the chords on the downbeats of measures 5 and 10.

In Memoriam: Alfred Eisner

Many of the Anniversaries are orchestral in conception, but perhaps none more so than this one, which comes across as a piano transcription of an orchestral sketch. One hears the sustained woodwind tones of the bare octaves at the opening, the *secco pizzicato* of the **ppp** chords in measures 5–7 (later played brutally by snare drums and *col legno* strings in measures 22–26), the warm string sound of the Coplandesque passages in measures 10–14 and later 27–33.

Bring out these different orchestral sounds through different attacks: full arm weight and strong wrists for woodwind octaves, grabbing (scratching!) notes with fingers for a *pizzicato* sound, and using full arm weight and loose wrists for a warm string sound. Play all with a flair for the dramatic. (To add to this sense of drama, Bernstein seems to quote the *Dies irae*, the Latin hymn associated with death, in measures 5–6 and 22–25).

One main technical difficulty of this piece occurs at the opening. Practice holding the octaves while playing the interior line *staccato*. This technique will ensure that you are releasing a note before moving on to the next one, more difficult to do when played *legato*. In the large octave leaps of measures 19–20, lead the large interval with your arm rather than your fingers. This technique will also assist you in achieving the directed *accelerando*, without which this passage becomes tedious.

Bernstein makes a stunning use of the *sostenuto* pedal beginning in measure 21. By holding the highest three Ds on the piano with the middle pedal, the *secco ff* chords that follow continually reactivate the high Ds through sympathetic vibrations of overtones, and what emerges is a distinctly un-piano-like sound of thin high tones sustained for far longer than is usually possible.

For Lukas Foss

Much of this piece places the two hands in close canon with one another. To bring out the effect, observe slurs and releases clearly. Phrase each hand as its own long line, leading the voicing with whichever hand states the melody first (the left hand in the opening, for example). Play the lead melodic lines with warmth and a sense of sustained sound (imagine a full string section playing—listen actively to the note all the way through until the end!). In measures 7–10 and 39–42 the right hand has the main line.

In measure 11, Bernstein marks *senza pedale*, "no pedal," but a tiny bit of pedal to ensure a smooth sound is a good idea (especially for performers with smaller hands who would struggle to connect the right-hand figures spanning a ninth). Pedal just a bit, but don't let the listener hear that you are pedaling! Measures 47–51 can be more obviously pedaled as we reach the denouement of the piece.

Measures 17–32 contain jumping octaves alternating with *scherzando* repeated notes. Keep arms and wrists loose in this passage. For the octaves, practice playing thumbs alone, and connecting the pairs of octaves in one gesture. Do not rush these passages!

In Memoriam: Ellen Goetz

Play this like a very slow Viennese waltz. A singing melodic line is required here, carefully balanced with both the bass line and the lilting second beats played in both hands. The second beats in particular should be played gracefully and *extremely* lightly—softer than you think! They should be less played than felt. Practice playing passages of the piece with the second beats "ghosted," or touched but not depressed. Then, barely add them back. Connect the top line through finger *legato* wherever possible.

This material was originally conceived of by Bernstein as a song for his mother titled "First Love (for My Mother, March 1986)," which was never published. The reported lyrics to measures 1–16 were: "My First Love, Jennie B., Eighty-Eight, young to me. My second love is eighty-eight too. Eighty-eight keys that sing to you…" Try singing those lyrics to get a sense for the length of the phrases, and the placement of breaths within the phrase.

The harmonic progression is sometimes surprising (example: the slide to D-flat major in measures 14–16). These shifts should be subtly highlighted through timing, voicing, tone color (but *not* through *crescendos*!). Play the two Cs in measures 32–33 differently from one another, like a flower that closes up at the end of the day.

In Memoriam: Nathalie Koussevitzky

Attention to clear voicing is particularly important in this Anniversary. The performer must project the melodic line in the right hand, balanced consistently with the lower voice in the same hand. Later, beginning at the end of measure 23, the voiced melody is the *lower* of the two voices, and is distributed between the hands. All lines should be played with abundant finger *legato*.

A sense of melancholy is highlighted by all the sighing motives, and the performer should play the piece with *rubato*, but without losing sight of the long phrases. A central challenge is bringing out the tremendous contrasts in register, dynamic, and mood without letting the piece become overly sectional.

The chord in measure 26 should not be rolled, if at all possible, in order to bring the music to an appropriately stark conclusion.

For Sergei Koussevitzky

Play this Anniversary with a sense of drama and a spoken, declamatory quality. It is crucial that the performer play *f* with accents while still maintaining a sense of line (i.e. do not bang!). Practice playing sections of the piece *legato* and *mp* to get a sense for the phrasing, and then re-impose the accents.

Voice tops of double-note passages, and use some pedal to ensure their connectedness. A large hand is necessary to play the chords in measures 4, 14 and 17; if possible, play these chords without rolling them.

For Susanna Kyle

This Anniversary should be played with the utmost simplicity and delicacy—hard to do well! The performer needs to find the right balance between projection and intimacy; perhaps consider the sound world of a Debussy prelude like *The Girl with the Flaxen Hair* as a reference point. Project a long line through all of the shifts in range, and make a clear distinction between *p* and *pp*.

The stops and starts in the phrasing should come across as reflective, not "counted." As a practice technique, try playing the phrases as if written in constant eighth notes (i.e. no waiting) and make a beautiful line. Introduce the reflective pauses while keeping the beautiful line you created when you played them as constant eighth notes. Listen closely to the ends of all notes!

The two voices in the left hand should always be connected via finger *legato*, with numerous finger substitutions throughout.

For Johnny Mehegan

True to its dedicatee, this Anniversary abounds in syncopations, rapid changes in register, and an astonishing variety of dynamic, phrase, and touch indications. The performer should pay careful attention to all of the specific markings in the score while playing with freewheeling abandon. Not an easy task! To capture that abandon, practice sections of the piece up to tempo (or close) as soon as possible after learning the basic note patterns. A long period in which one plays the piece at half tempo will absolutely destroy any sense of the *joie de vivre* of the music.

Although the piece is in common time, the underlying pulse is the characteristic rhumba rhythm: ♩. ♩. ♩

Practice clapping the rhythm, tapping it out on the keyboard lid, whatever it takes to internalize the syncopation as *the* basic pulse of the piece. Observe silences (measures 6, 7, 12, 18, 23) precisely!

Rapid double thirds (measures 5, 17) can be practiced using the following method: play the thirds at one-quarter tempo with all top notes played *legato* and bottom notes *staccatissimo*. Top notes should all be connected through finger *legato*. When you return to full tempo, keep the top notes connected while allowing for a slightly detached articulation in the bottom notes.

For Felicia Montealegre

The main melodic material has an almost folk-like simplicity, and should be played with a singing tone and without much *rubato*. The translation of Bernstein's performance direction *piacevole* into the English "pleasant" or "agreeable" doesn't quite capture the full sense of the Italian word. The music should be played in a graceful, warm way and without an excess of passion. It has a similar meaning to the performance direction *grazioso*. Use pedal but do not let melodic notes blur together. As a result, finger *legato* is essential to maintaining that singing quality, with numerous finger substitutions ensuring that melodic notes are well-connected.

The middle section of the piece presents the additional challenge of connecting a *legatissimo* octave melody with a busy accompaniment of unison sixteenth notes in both hands. Play the sixteenth notes as softly as possible so the octave line comes out. To connect the octaves, use no more than a quarter pedal, and flutter pedal as you move your hand between octave positions so as to not blur the sixteenth-note line. Practice this by playing the passage at half tempo and playing the sixteenth notes *staccatissimo* while connecting the octaves with small bursts of pedal.

When the opening melody returns in measure 31, be sure to voice the melody well above the right-hand accompaniment.

For Shirley Gabis Rhoads Perle

The rhythmic profile of this Anniversary shares that of a Baroque sarabande, with its stately emphasis on the second beat. Make sure to feel the weight of the second beats *without* stopping the flow of the phrase; keep your wrist and arm in motion even as you hold the long notes in the middle of each bar. Practice playing the melodic line as all quarter notes (i.e. no dotted rhythms or held notes) to get a sense for the line, and keep that line at all costs once you reintroduce the written rhythms.

The top lines should be connected wherever possible through the judicious use of pedal and, especially, finger *legato*. Voice to the top always in this piece. Pace yourself—there are only two phrases in this entire piece (measures 1–8 and 9–17). Know where you want the highs and lows of each phrase to be, and project them clearly.

For Elizabeth Rudolf

A Brahmsian *grazioso* seems to be Bernstein's inspiration here, almost like a waltz in 2/4 time. Keep arms loose so as to phrase fluidly through all the starts and stops of the line. The phrases should sound graceful, like a ballet dancer fluently connecting together *pliés* and *relevés* to create an overall gesture.

In measure 22, a second voice enters, melancholically. Voice the higher melody much more strongly than the continuing lilting phrase beneath, as if occupying a different emotional sphere. Practice the right hand using the following technique: play the top melodic notes connected with great finger *legato*, and play the lower notes *staccatissimo*. Alternatively, you could "ghost" the lower notes (i.e. play them silently). The top voice should be connected at all costs using finger substitutions. Imagine that your fourth and fifth fingers are made of platinum, while your lower fingers are wet noodles.

Measures 17–46 are in the unusual key of C-sharp major; take care to check the key signature to make sure you are playing the correct notes!

The texture thins considerably beginning in measure 56. Bernstein marks *cantando* in measure 58, and this applies to the rest of the piece. Play the right-hand notes voiced, as if pressing the key down through the keybed and to the floor, but with loose arms (arm weight). This will produce the necessary projected *pianissimo* sound.

For William Schuman

As in "For Sergei Koussevitzky," play this piece *f* with accents but while still maintaining a sense of the line. Practice sections *legato* and *mp* to determine the contours of the phrasing. In performance, individual notes should be etached and incisive but not overly *staccato*. Use a combination of arm weight and finger strength to achieve this effect.

Keep an ironclad sense of pulse throughout this piece—do not push forward until the *Più mosso* is indicated! A strong pulse is particularly important from measures 27–33. Practice with a metronome, beginning below tempo, and build tempo up to the performance indication. Double notes beginning in measure 16 pose a particular challenge; play these with an extremely loose wrist so as to bounce between the notes.

For Leo Smit

From his student days at Harvard, Bernstein wrote admiringly of Prokofiev's music.[6] Fifty years later, he wrote this Anniversary, strongly reminiscent of Prokofiev's compositional language, and perhaps most closely akin to that older composer's *Visions Fugitives*. Play this piece with a biting articulation, mostly from the fingers and wrist. Keep that same articulation even when the material is repeated *p*.

Finger independence is important to achieve the rapid 1-2-3-4-5 and 5-4-3-2-1 figures called for in this piece while clearly hearing every note. Several traditional method books, such as those by Czerny and Hanon, can help in this regard. Keep a strong sense of pulse throughout (while brooking no change in pulse whatsoever when the music gets softer!). Rests in particular should be precisely observed, and Do Not Rush!

For Stephen Sondheim

Many parts of this graceful *andantino* feel delicately suspended in mid-air. Bernstein's use of a bass note stuck on the fifth scale degree (rather than the more settled tonic) contributes to this effect, as do the constant shifts in rhythm that obscure the written 3/4 time signature. Play these shifts subtly, with a sense of unhurried wandering, as if improvising.

Hold all notes for their full rhythmic value, which will mean keeping careful track of when fingers need to come off keys, and a fair number of finger substitutions. Make a clear distinction between *p* and *pp*. As if to emphasize its waywardness, the music pauses every three bars or so; be careful to pace yourself so that the piece holds together.

On the last line, Bernstein indicates four chords to be played preceded by a breath mark. By marking the chords on the second eighth note of each bar, Bernstein indicates an upbeat-style attack on each chord. Each chord should be shaded differently to highlight the shifting registers and harmonies.

---

6   See, for example, "New Music in Boston," reprinted in *Findings*.

For Craig Urquhart

The primary challenges in this short graceful dance lie in holding notes while playing *scherzando* figures in the same hand, and in projecting a singing line in one hand while the other jokingly insists on a short, *staccato* articulation. To achieve the latter, use finger *legato* almost exclusively throughout the piece. You should be able to play the entire piece with no pedal at all, and then add it back in only when you absolutely cannot live without it. Notice that the piece is in cut time; the half note has the beat. Play the piece in two, not four.

THANK YOUS

For their support at various stages of this project, I am grateful to Mary Van De Loo, Instructor of Piano Pedagogy at Lawrence University; Katherine Baber, Associate Professor of Music History at the University of Redlands; Sigrid Luther, Professor Emeritus of Music at Bryan College in Dayton, Tennessee; Leann Osterkamp; Gianna Santino, my student at Lawrence University who assisted me in trying out fingerings for this edition; and, especially, Richard Walters, Vice President of Classical and Vocal Publications at Hal Leonard LLC, and Joshua Parman, my editor at Hal Leonard. Finally, I would like to thank my wife, Erica Scheinberg, for providing insightful feedback throughout the project.

FOR FURTHER READING

Bernstein, Leonard. *Findings*. New York: Simon and Schuster, 1982.

_____. *The Infinite Variety of Music*. New York: Simon and Schuster, 1962.

_____. *The Joy of Music*. New York: Simon and Schuster, 1959.

Burton, Humphrey. *Leonard Bernstein*. New York: Doubleday, 1994.

Chapin, Schuyler. *Leonard Bernstein: Notes from a Friend*. New York: Walker and Company, 1992.

Luther, Sigrid. "The Anniversaries for Solo Piano by Leonard Bernstein." DMA document, Louisiana State University, 1986.

Peyser, Joan. *Bernstein: A Biography, Revised and Updated*. New York: Billboard Books, 1998.

Secrest, Meryle. *Leonard Bernstein: A Life*. New York: Random House, Inc., 1994.

RECORDINGS OF THE ANNIVERSARIES

(As of January, 2018)

Dossin, Alexander. *Bernstein: Thirteen Anniversaries*. Naxos 8.559756, 2015, compact disc.

Laimon, Sara. *American Piano Works of the 1940s*. Albany TROY685, 2004, compact disc.

Lanner, Thomas. *Touches of Bernstein: The Complete Published Piano Music of Leonard Bernstein*. Centaur CRC 2702, 2004, compact disc.

Lee, Warren. *Touches and Traces: Piano Music by Leonard Bernstein and Tan Dun*. Naxos 9.70252, 2016, compact disc.

Osterkamp, Leann. *The Complete Piano Works of Leonard Bernstein*. Steinway & Sons, 2017, compact disc.

IN MEMORIAM: ELLEN GOETZ
(June 16, 1930–January 27, 1986)
from *Thirteen Anniversaries*

LEONARD BERNSTEIN

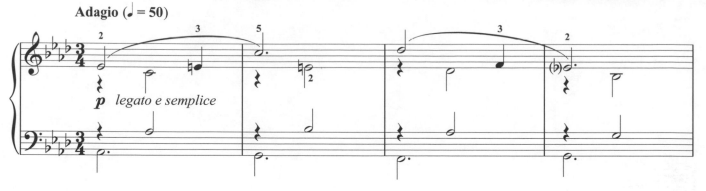

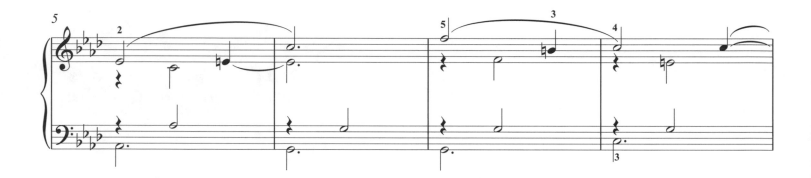

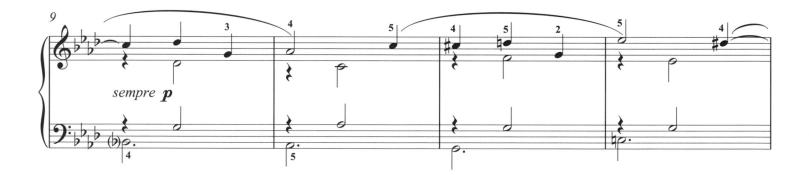

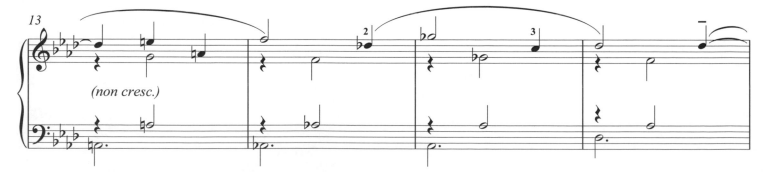

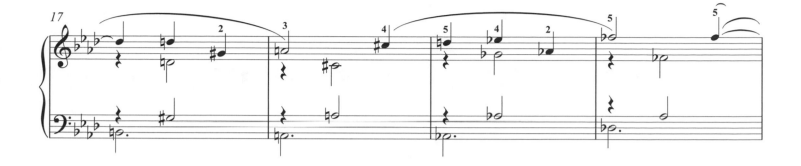

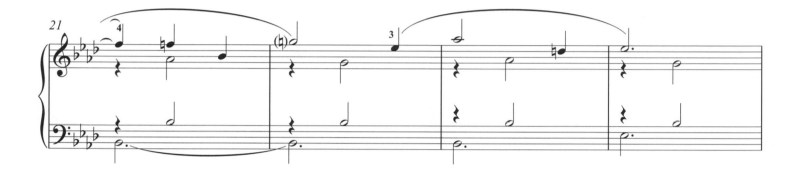

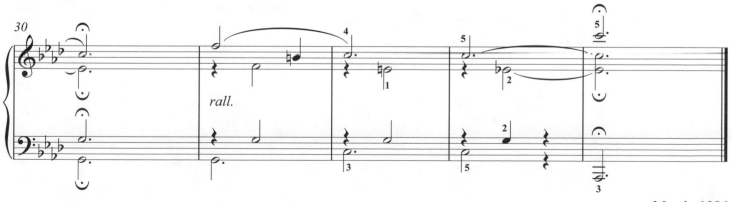

March, 1986

FOR SHIRLEY GABIS RHOADS PERLE

(born April 7, 1924)

from *Thirteen Anniversaries*

LEONARD BERNSTEIN

Related Online
Video Piano Lesson
2

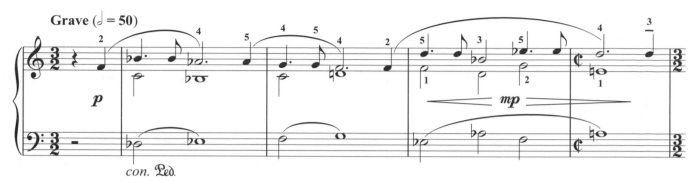

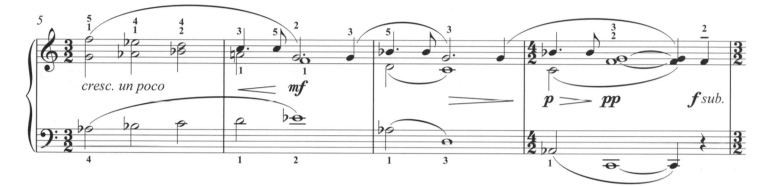

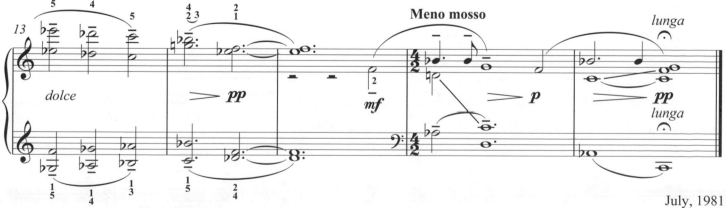

July, 1981

IN MEMORIAM: HELEN COATES
(July 19, 1899–February 27, 1989)
from *Thirteen Anniversaries*

LEONARD BERNSTEIN

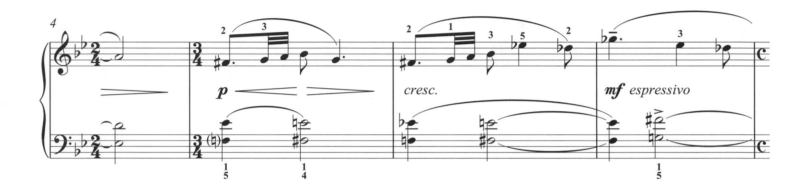

17 July 1970**

*Please refer to Historical and Pedagogical Commentary (page 10) for pedaling options in these passages.
**This music originally appeared as part of *Mass*, written in 1970.

Related Online
Video Piano Lesson
6

FOR LEO SMIT
(born January 12, 1921)
from *Thirteen Anniversaries*

LEONARD BERNSTEIN

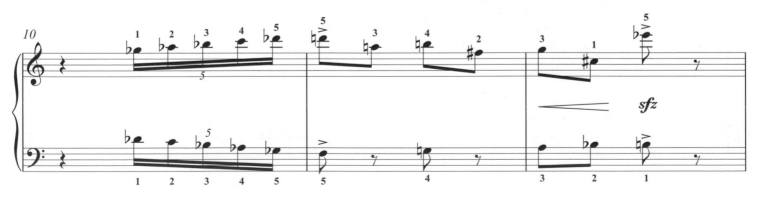

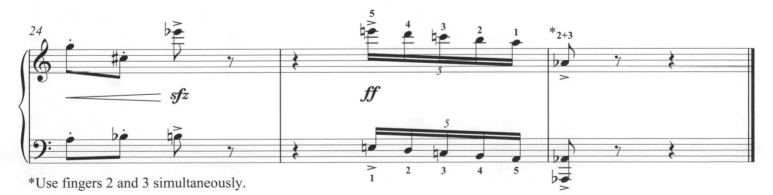

*Use fingers 2 and 3 simultaneously.

5 February 1988

FOR SUSANNA KYLE

(born July 24, 1949)

from *Five Anniversaries*

LEONARD BERNSTEIN

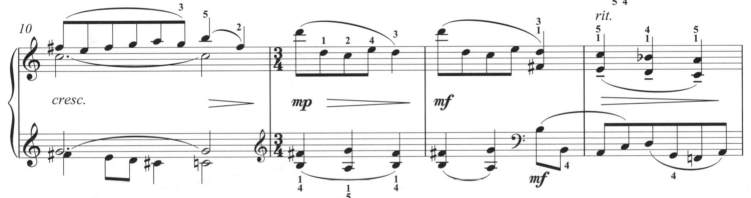

As at first, but slower

Much slower

FOR STEPHEN SONDHEIM
(born March 22, 1930)
from *Thirteen Anniversaries*

LEONARD BERNSTEIN

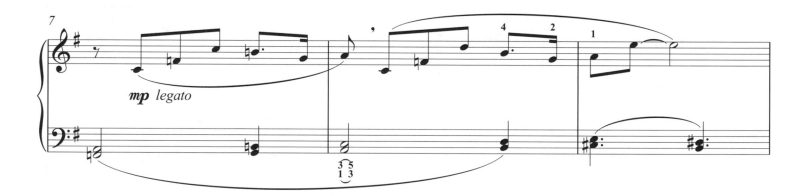

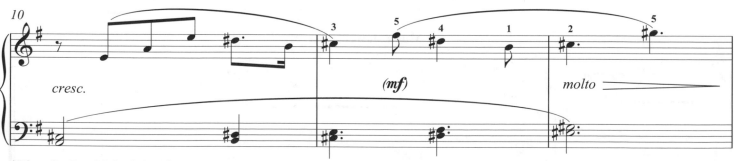

*Play the D with both hands.

Meno mosso (quasi lento)

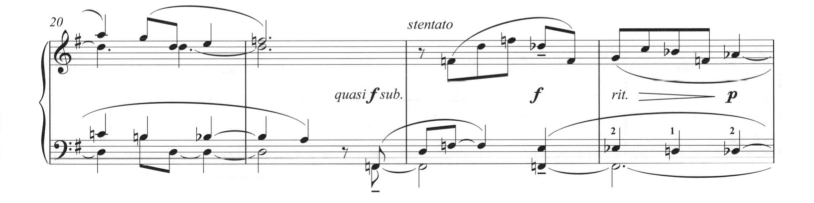

Tempo primo

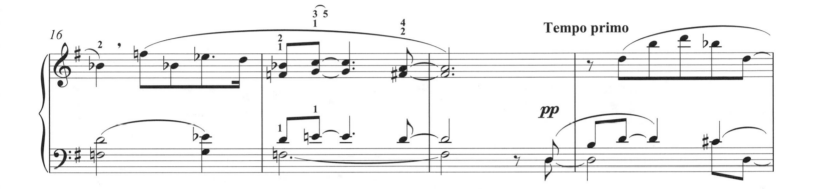

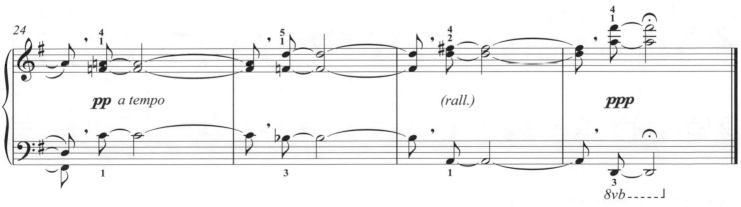

20 March 1965

Related Online
Video Piano Lesson
9

FOR ELIZABETH RUDOLF
(born January 23, 1894)
from *Five Anniversaries*

LEONARD BERNSTEIN

Allegretto (♩ = 126)

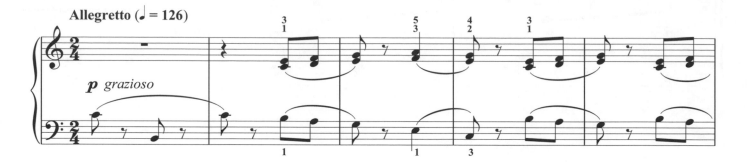

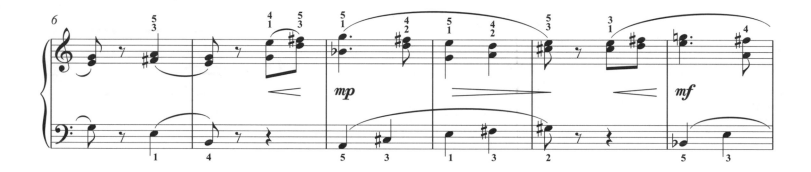

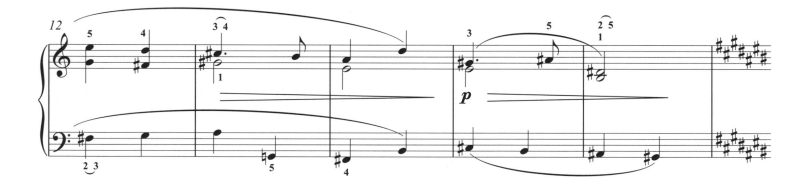

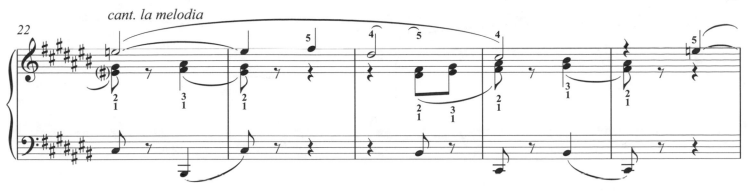

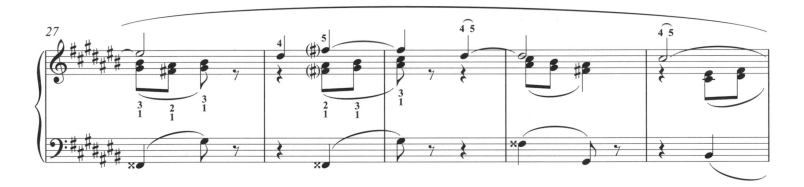

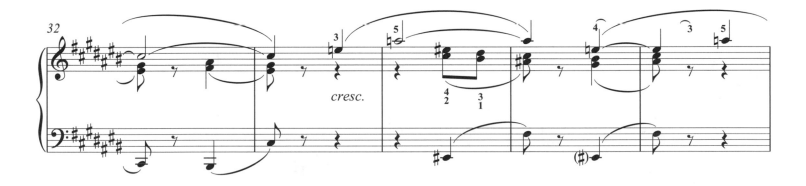

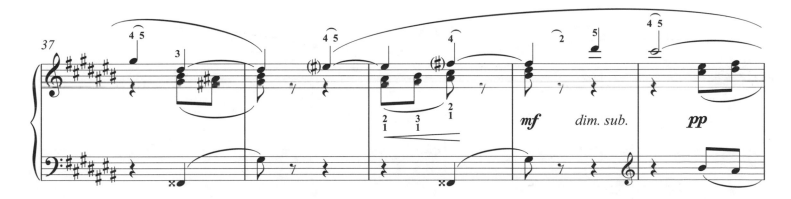

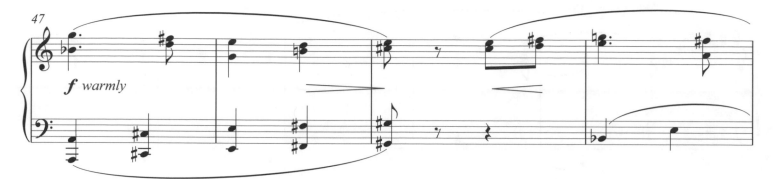

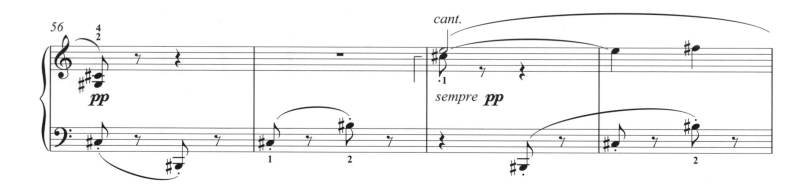

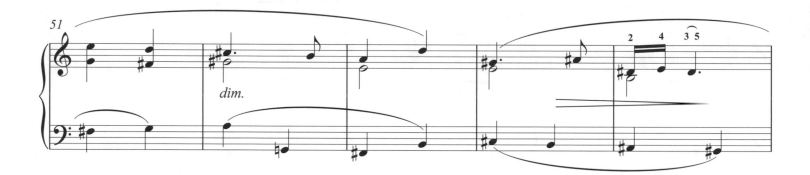

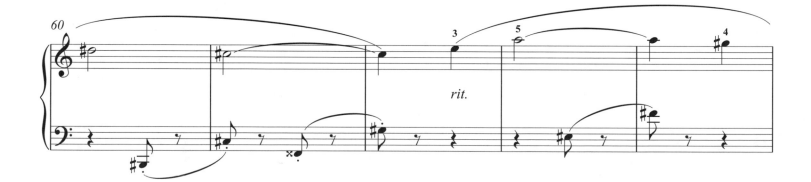

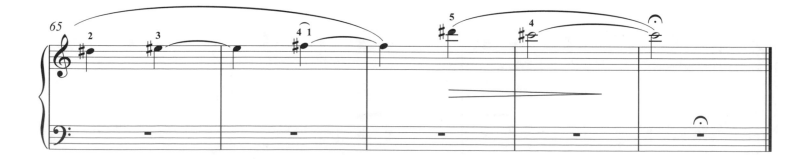

FOR LUKAS FOSS
(born August 15, 1922)
from *Five Anniversaries*

Related Online
Video Piano Lesson
3

LEONARD BERNSTEIN

Allegro con anima (♩ = 132)

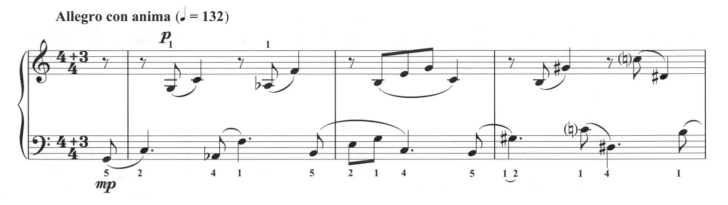

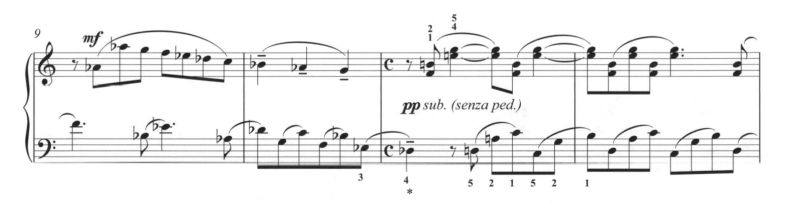

*Please refer to Historical and Pedagogical Commentary (page 11) for a discussion of pedaling in this passage.

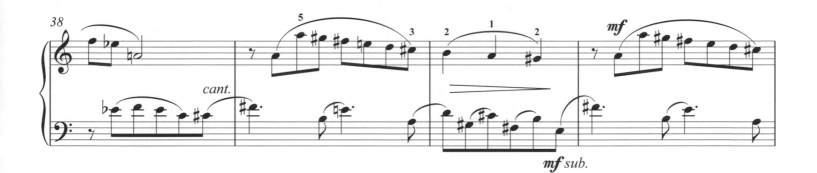

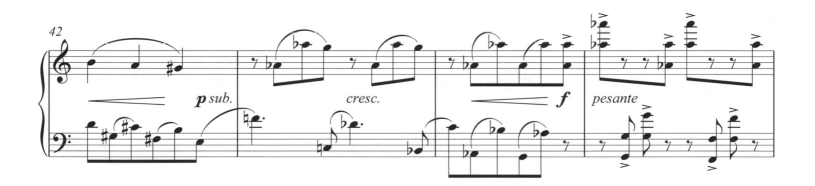

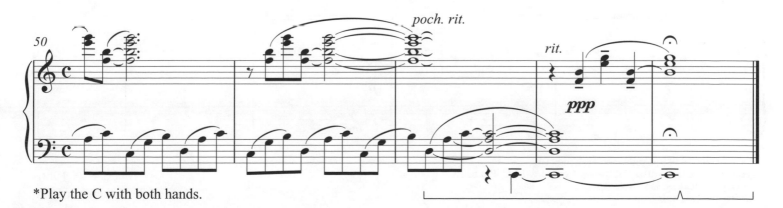

*Play the C with both hands.

FOR CRAIG URQUHART

(born September 3, 1953)

from *Thirteen Anniversaries*

LEONARD BERNSTEIN

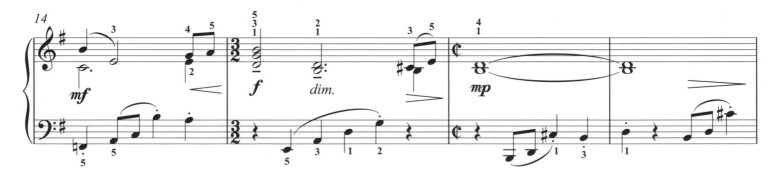

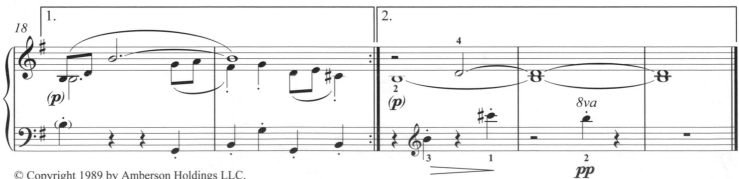

1960s
revised 25 November 1986

Related Online
Video Piano Lessons
3 and 4

FOR AARON COPLAND

(born November 14, 1900)

from *Seven Anniversaries*

LEONARD BERNSTEIN

Allegretto semplice (♩ = 108)

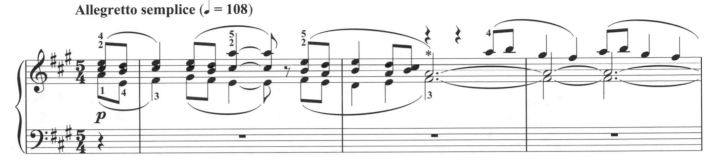

*Strike the A with finger 1 in the right hand; substitute for finger 1 in the left hand to hold the note.

Related Online
Video Piano Lessons
1 and 7

IN MEMORIAM: ALFRED EISNER

(died January 4, 1941)

from *Seven Anniversaries*

LEONARD BERNSTEIN

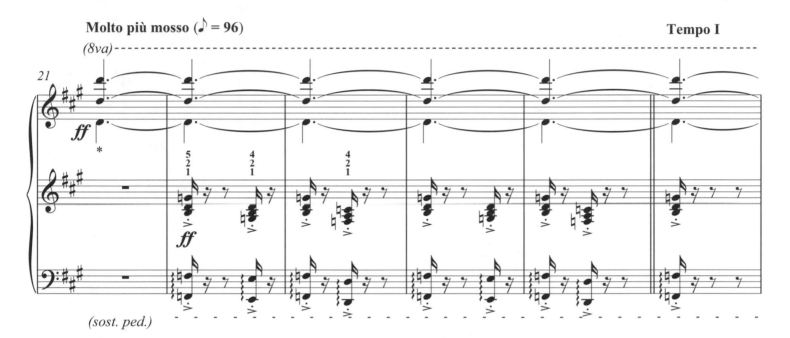

Molto più mosso (♪ = 96) Tempo I

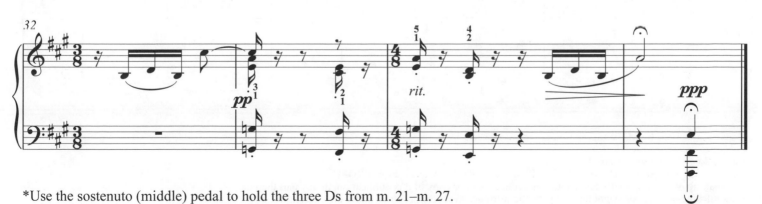

*Use the sostenuto (middle) pedal to hold the three Ds from m. 21–m. 27.

IN MEMORIAM: NATHALIE KOUSSEVITZKY
(died January 15, 1942)

LEONARD BERNSTEIN

from *Seven Anniversaries*

Related Online Video
Piano Lessons 4 and 8

Lento non troppo (♩ = 50)

FOR SERGEI KOSSEVITZKY

(born July 26, 1874)

from *Seven Anniversaries*

LEONARD BERNSTEIN

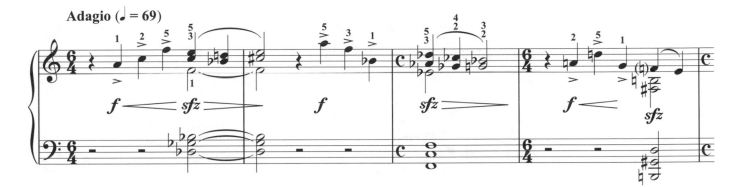

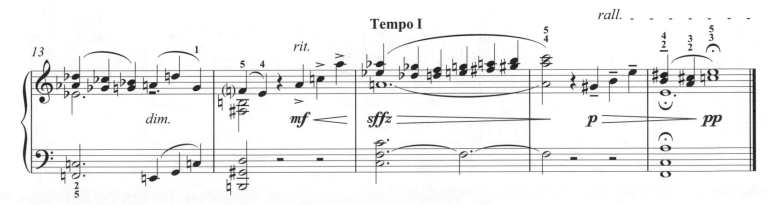

Related Online
Video Piano Lesson
2

FOR WILLIAM SCHUMAN

(born August 4, 1910)

from *Seven Anniversaries*

LEONARD BERNSTEIN

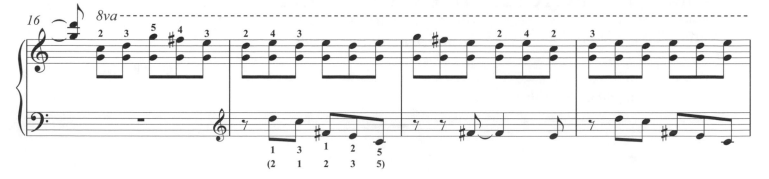

Related Online
Video Piano Lessons
3, 4, and 10

FOR FELICIA MONTEALEGRE

(born February 6, 1922)

from *Four Anniversaries*

LEONARD BERNSTEIN

Tranquillo: piacevole (♪ = 88)

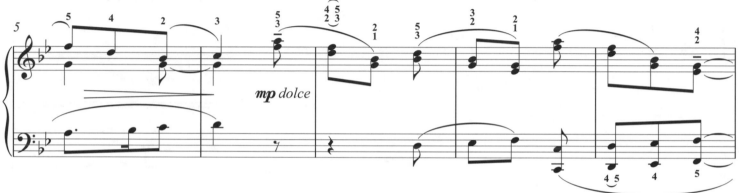

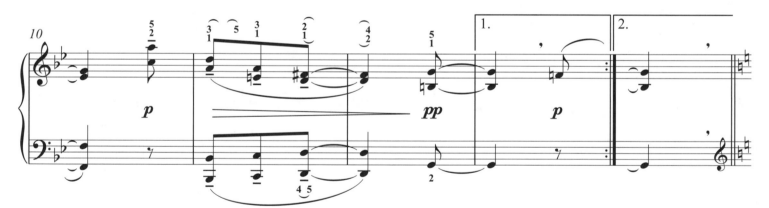

Pochiss. più mosso

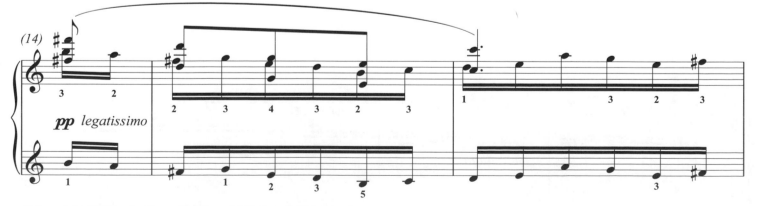

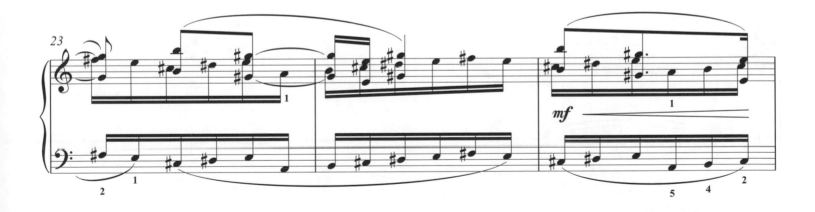

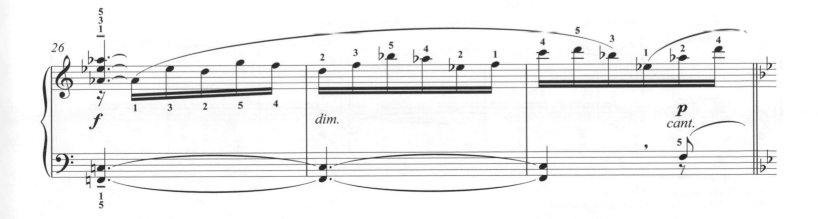

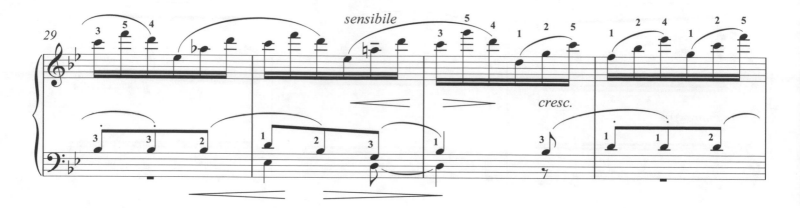

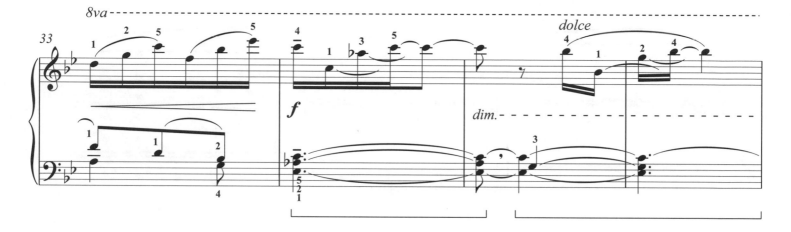

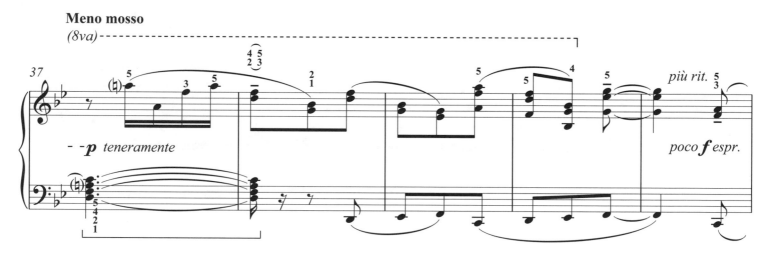

Related Online
Video Piano Lessons
2 and 11

FOR JOHNNY MEHEGAN
(born June 6, 1920)
from *Four Anniversaries*

LEONARD BERNSTEIN

Agitato: scherzando (♩ = 176) [♩ = 176–192]

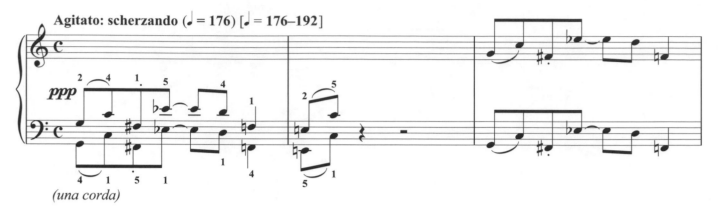

(una corda)

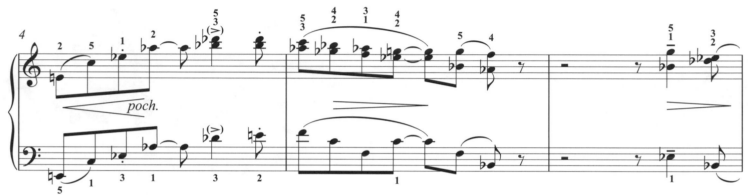

(tre corde)

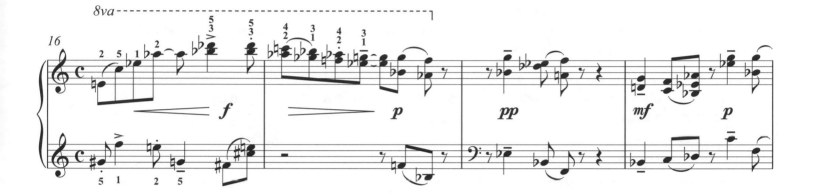

Praised as "intrepid" (*Philadelphia Inquirer*), "engaging" (*Houston Chronicle*), and "endlessly fascinating" (WQXR New York), pianist **Michael Mizrahi** has won acclaim for his compelling performances of a wide-ranging repertoire and his ability to connect with audiences of all ages. He has appeared as concerto soloist, recitalist, chamber musician, and teaching artist across the United States and abroad.

Mr. Mizrahi has performed in the world's leading concert halls including Carnegie Hall, Toyko's Suntory Hall, the Kimmel Center in Philadelphia, Jordan Hall and the Gardner Museum in Boston, the Kennedy Center in Washington, DC, the Chicago Cultural Center and Houston's Jones Hall. He has performed as soloist with the Houston Symphony, National Symphony, Haddonfield Symphony, Sioux City Symphony, and Prince Georges Philharmonic, among others. He has given solo recitals at the Phillips Collection in Washington, DC and has made repeated appearances on the Dame Myra Hess Concert Series in Chicago. His chamber music festival appearances include Music@Menlo, Verbier, the Yellow Barn Music Festival, and the Steans Institute at the Ravinia Festival. Mr. Mizrahi won First Prize and the Audience Choice Award in the Ima Hogg International Competition, as well as first prizes in the International Bartók-Kabalevsky Competition and the Iowa International Piano Competition. He won third prize in the San Antonio International Piano Competition. Mr. Mizrahi appeared for many years on the active roster of Astral Artists.

Recognized widely for his commitment to artistic excellence, Michael Mizrahi won Lawrence University's 2013 Award for Excellence in Creative Activity, and, in 2014, was one of five international recipients of the S&R Foundation's Washington Award.

An enthusiastic promoter of music education, Mizrahi has presented lecture-recitals and master classes at the University of North Carolina – Chapel Hill, the University of Redlands, the University of California – San Diego, the American School in Switzerland (TASIS), and the University of Nebraska at Omaha, among many others. As a member of Carnegie Hall's prestigious *Academy* program (now *Ensemble Connect*) and *Teaching Artists Collaborative*, Mr. Mizrahi spent several years as a teaching artist in New York City public schools.

Dedicated to the music of our time, Mr. Mizrahi has commissioned and given world premieres of several new works by today's leading composers, including Missy Mazzoli, Judd Greenstein, Sarah Kirkland Snider, Mark Dancigers, and John Luther Adams. He is a founding member of NOW Ensemble, a chamber group devoted to the commissioning and performing of new music by emerging composers. Mr. Mizrahi's celebrated albums *The Bright Motion* and *Currents*, both albums of new solo piano works commissioned by Mizrahi, were released on the New Amsterdam Records label. His popular music videos have been lauded by *National Public Radio* and *New Yorker* music critic Alex Ross. Mr. Mizrahi co-directs the New Music @ Lawrence concert series.

Mr. Mizrahi is also a member of Decoda, a chamber ensemble comprised of virtuoso musicians, entrepreneurs, and passionate advocates of the arts. Based in New York City, Decoda creates innovative performances and engaging projects with partners around the world. Mr. Mizrahi teaches each summer at the prestigious Decoda Skidmore Chamber Music Institute. Drawing from his work with Decoda, Mizrahi has worked to foster partnerships between Lawrence University's Conservatory of Music and the surrounding community, and helped found Lawrence's *Music For All* project that brings classical chamber music to children and populations who ordinarily do not participate.

Mr. Mizrahi has edited several new editions published by Hal Leonard, including new editions of piano music by Ginastera, Bernstein, and Chopin.

Michael Mizrahi received his bachelor's degree from the University of Virginia, where his concentrations were in music, religion and physics. He holds master's and doctoral degrees from the Yale School of Music, where he studied with Claude Frank. As a member of the Moët Trio, Mr. Mizrahi completed a two-year residency, the only one of its kind for piano trios, at the New England Conservatory.

After his Philadelphia debut recital, the *Philadelphia Inquirer* wrote that "…the performance had transparency, revealing a forward-moving logic and chord voices you didn't previously realize were there…textures were sumptuous."

He is Associate Professor of Piano at the Lawrence University Conservatory of Music in Appleton, Wisconsin. For more information, please visit michaelmizrahipiano.com.